EMMITT SMITH

EMMITT SMITH

Relentless Rusher

Stew Thornley

Lerner Publications Company
Minneapolis

Information in this book came from the following sources:
1995 Dallas Cowboy Media Guide, The Associated Press, *Current Biography, Dallas Morning News,* National High School Sports Record Book, *Science World, Sport* magazine, *Sports Illustrated, St. Petersburg Times, The Sporting News, The Sporting News* Pro Football Register, University of Florida Football Media Guide, and Emmitt Smith's 1994 autobiography, *The Emmitt Zone,* co-written by Steve Delsohn and published by Taylor Publishing Company.

This book is available in two editions:
Library binding by Lerner Publications Company
Soft cover by First Avenue Editions
241 First Avenue North
Minneapolis, Minnesota 55401

LIBRARY OF CONGRESS CATALOGING-IN-PUBLICATION DATA

Thornley, Stew.
    Emmitt Smith : relentless rusher / Stew Thornley.
      p.   cm.
    Summary: Profiles the star running back who helped the Dallas Cowboys win Super Bowls in 1993, 1994, and 1996.
    ISBN 0-8225-2897-5 (alk. paper). — ISBN 0-8225-9747-0 (pbk. : alk. paper)
    1. Smith, Emmitt, 1969–   —Juvenile literature.   2. Football players—United States—Biography—Juvenile literature.   3. Dallas Cowboys (Football team)—Juvenile literature. [1. Smith, Emmitt, 1969– . 2. Football players. 3. Afro-Americans—Biography. 4. Dallas Cowboys (Football team)]   I. Title.
GV939.S635T56   1997
796.332'092—dc20
[B]   96–7799

Manufactured in the United States of America
2 3 4 5 6 – JR – 02 01 00 99 98 97

Contents

Emmitt celebrates after scoring the game's first touchdown against the New York Giants.

A One-Armed Gang

A lot was on the line for the Dallas Cowboys in their final game of the 1993 regular season. They were tied for first place in the National Football Conference (NFC) Eastern Division with the team they were playing, the New York Giants. Both teams would advance to the playoffs no matter who won the game. But the loser would go as a wild-card team and have to play again the following week. The winner would get a week off and have the home field advantage on the road to the Super Bowl.

The Cowboys' star running back, Emmitt Smith, had a personal stake in the game. He was trying to lead the National Football League (NFL) in rushing for the third straight year. Only three players—Steve Van Buren, Jim Brown, and Earl Campbell—had ever done that. Emmitt really wanted the rushing title, partly because of the way the season began.

He had missed the Cowboys' first two games in a contract dispute. After Emmitt's old contract ended, he and team owner Jerry Jones hadn't agreed on a new one. The negotiations carried on for months. At one point, Jones questioned Emmitt's value to the team by saying, "Emmitt is a luxury, not a necessity, for the Cowboys."

When the Cowboys lost their first two games without Emmitt, Jones quickly learned the running back *was* a necessity for the Cowboys to win.

Emmitt isn't the biggest or the fastest running back in football. Experts have talked about the qualities he *does* have that make him so good. One is great vision, which allows him to see the whole field. As he lines up, he can see nearly all the players on both teams. He can also anticipate the action. "It's not a blur, but a clear picture," he says. "I can usually look at a defense and predict where the hole will be, regardless of where the play is called."

If the hole isn't where Emmitt expects it to be, he can cut quickly to find another route. Although he doesn't have the greatest "straight-ahead speed," he is known for his terrific "change-of-direction" speed.

Emmitt's tremendous strength, both in his massive thighs and his powerful upper body, is another asset. Other qualities that contribute to his greatness are desire and determination. "If you want to get through a hole bad enough, you'll get through it," he says.

Few running backs have Emmitt's combination of talents. He changes directions very quickly, yet keeps an eye on what's happening all around him.

He is also durable. Running backs endure a lot of punishment from crushing tackles. Few backs in the NFL carry the ball more than Emmitt. No matter how hard the hit, he almost always gets up.

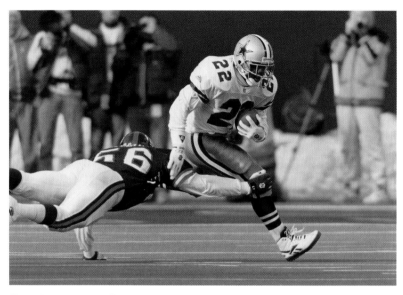

Emmitt eludes Giant linebacker Lawrence Taylor on a first-half run.

In the game against the Giants, though, Emmitt's durability received a real test. Late in the first half, he broke through a hole for a 46-yard run. New York safety Greg Jackson finally stopped him with a tackle that slammed his right shoulder into the hard turf at Giants Stadium. Emmitt's shoulder separated. "The pain was so bad I couldn't describe it," Emmitt later said. The run set up a field goal that gave Dallas a 13–0 lead as the first half ended.

In the locker room at halftime, trainer Kevin O'Neill asked Emmitt if he thought he'd be going back into the game.

"I'm not coming out," Emmitt said. "I've got to play."

After Emmitt's injury, winning the game was even more important for the Cowboys. Emmitt would have more time to heal if Dallas didn't play the next week. The trainer patched up Emmitt as best he could. He put a harness under his shoulder pad and a thigh pad over it to provide extra protection. He then used an elastic bandage to hold everything—including Emmitt's shoulder—together.

The third quarter had already started when Emmitt returned to the sideline. The Giants were staging a comeback and soon cut the Cowboy lead to 13–7. Emmitt's arm motion was limited, but he went back into the game. Quarterback Troy Aikman lowered his handoffs so Emmitt would have an easier time taking the ball.

But Emmitt was more concerned about the hits he was taking. "Guys, whenever I get tackled, someone has to help me up," he said to his teammates in the huddle.

As much as he could, he kept his right arm close to his body and he hugged the ball with his left arm. But when he had to reach up for a pass or out to push away a would-be tackler, he used the injured arm, despite the intense pain.

Often he walked off the field with his arm hanging limply by his side. The fans figured he was through. But within a few plays, Emmitt would be back.

11

New York scored another touchdown, and the teams were tied 13–13 when time ran out. The game went into sudden-death overtime. The first team to score would win. The Giants received the kickoff but couldn't advance the ball. They punted to the Cowboys, who started a drive on their own 25-yard line. In the next 11 plays, Emmitt either caught or carried the ball 9 times. On his final carry, he darted through the left side of the line for a 10-yard gain, advancing the ball to the New York 24. Eddie Murray came in and kicked a field goal to win the game for Dallas.

After the game, though, the focus was on Emmitt and his gutsy play. "Smith's performance . . . should be remembered as one of the great individual efforts in league history," wrote Chris Mortensen in *The Sporting News*.

Emmitt finished the game with 168 yards on 32 carries, with 13 of those carries coming after the painful injury. Emmitt left Giants Stadium with his arm in a sling. On the flight home, he heard the good news that he had won the NFL rushing championship for the third year in a row.

Emmitt was voted the NFL Most Valuable Player for the 1993 season. A few weeks later, he led the Cowboys to their second-straight Super Bowl championship with a 30–13 win over the Buffalo Bills.

But the game that stayed in people's minds was his incredible performance against the Giants in the final regular-season game. "The best way to measure a great player is how he performs under the toughest of conditions," Dallas coach Jimmy Johnson said. "With Emmitt, no matter what it is—a bad field due to the weather, a quality defense he's facing, a painful injury he's having to overcome—you see the greatness.

"He's not fancy and there's no frills, but the results say it all."

Emmitt during his junior year of high school

14

Young Sensation

During the 1970s, the Dallas Cowboys had one of the best teams in the NFL. They were on national television often and developed a following outside of Dallas. The Cowboys became known as "America's Team" because they had so many fans across the country. One of those fans was a young boy in the panhandle region of Florida.

As Emmitt Smith III grew up in Pensacola, his heroes were Dallas stars Roger Staubach and Tony Dorsett. He dreamed about someday playing for the Dallas Cowboys.

Emmitt was born May 15, 1969. His parents, Mary and Emmitt II, knew he had both the interest and the physical ability to become a great football star. When Emmitt was only nine months old, Mary placed him in his crib and went into another room to watch television. A few minutes later, she was surprised to see her baby crawling past. Emmitt had climbed from his crib—at an age when many babies are just learning to pull themselves to a standing position!

Another time Mary placed Emmitt in his baby swing. She noticed that Emmitt paid close attention to a football game airing on the television.

The Smith family wasn't rich. Emmitt II drove a city bus. Mary stayed at home for many years to raise Emmitt and his siblings. Until Emmitt was eight, the Smiths lived in a government housing project.

Emmitt's father had been an outstanding athlete, starring in both football and basketball at Washington High School in Pensacola. As Emmitt grew, he showed similar athletic talent. He had great balance and enjoyed walking on narrow curbs and fences. Long bike rides around Pensacola helped him build leg strength and stamina. "I was fortunate my dad was such a great athlete," he once said. "I guess I got my athletic ability from him."

Emmitt's parents strongly encouraged the children to work hard in school. "Education is something you'll have until the day you die," Emmitt II told all his children.

When Emmitt's family moved out of the government projects, their new home was right behind Emmitt II's parents. Emmitt helped care for his bedridden grandmother. A few years later, he worked at a nursing home and enjoyed assisting the residents.

As a child, Emmitt was always big for his age. His mother made sure to carry his birth certificate so she could prove he wasn't too old to play in certain leagues.

By the time Emmitt was 11, he was moving up to higher level leagues to play with older kids. Even then, he ran into weight restrictions. When Emmitt was 13 and couldn't play in a league because he weighed too much, his head coach made him an assistant coach and put him in charge of the team's running backs.

Emmitt played in youth leagues because the school he attended in seventh and eighth grade did not have a football program. Instead, he played basketball and ran for the track team at Brownsville Middle School. The Brownsville basketball team won the city championship in Emmitt's first year on the team.

Emmitt spent most of his time playing sports or doing schoolwork, which also kept him away from temptations such as alcohol and other drugs. "I saw drugs in the projects but never even experimented with them," he said. In fact, before he finished high school, he even represented the nation's high school football players at the White House as part of President Reagan's "Say No to Drugs" campaign.

When Emmitt reached the ninth grade, he began attending Escambia High School. The Escambia Gators football team had finished with a record of one win and nine losses the year before and had managed only one winning season over the previous 18 years.

In 1983 the Gators had a new coach, Dwight Thomas. Thomas had been a successful coach at Choctawhatchee High School in Fort Walton Beach, Florida. But he was fired because the team had never won a state championship with him as coach. Angry, Thomas vowed to take over a losing football program and lead it to success. Escambia seemed to be a good place to do this, especially with a young player like Emmitt about to join.

When Emmitt's freshman season began, Thomas handed out cards to the players so they could write down what they hoped to achieve. "It's a dream until you write it down," Thomas told the players. "Then it's a goal."

Emmitt thought about what he wanted to do, then wrote down his goal: to rush for more than 1,500 yards in a season.

He got off to a good start in his first game, running for 115 yards and two touchdowns against Pensacola Catholic High. Opponents quickly learned how tough it was to stop the Gators' new running ace. "Emmitt just kind of scoots his feet along; that's the reason he never gets knocked off balance," said Escambia assistant coach Jimmy Nichols. "He looks at the defense and has a knack for anticipating where the pressure is going to come from."

Escambia's star running back, Emmitt, picks up some yardage on his way to 1,500 for the season.

Following his blocker, Emmitt scoots along in a 1986 game against Clarksville (Tennessee) Northeast High School. He gained 132 yards in the game, which Escambia won.

Eventually the defensive players on opposing teams showed up with a 24—Emmitt's number—taped to their helmets. It was their way of announcing who their target was.

Football was a family affair for the Smiths. Mary, employed at a bank when the children were in school, would stop on her way home to watch Emmitt practice. For the actual games, the entire family would be in the stands. But Emmitt wasn't the only one in the family playing football. Emmitt's brother Emory played in a Saturday morning youth league, using the same field Emmitt did. Then on Saturday night the Smiths would return again to the Escambia High field, this time to watch 40-year-old Emmitt II play for the Pensacola Wings in the semi-professional Dixie League.

Led by Emmitt, the Escambia Gators went 7–3 in 1983—a big improvement from the previous year. The team did even better in Emmitt's sophomore season. So did Emmitt. He rushed for nearly 1,900 yards as the Gators went 9–2 in the regular season. He would have gained even more yardage, but Coach Thomas pulled most of the starters once the game was safely in hand. In some games, Emmitt had fewer than 10 carries before coming out. He never complained, even though he loved to play. Instead, he became the team's biggest cheerleader from the sideline.

As the season progressed, Emmitt saw the recruiting letters an older teammate was receiving from different colleges. Emmitt wondered if he would someday get scholarship offers from colleges wanting him to play football for them.

In the meantime, he concentrated on playing for Escambia. With their fine record, the Gators advanced to the state playoffs. Emmitt averaged nearly 180 yards a game as Escambia won three games and the Florida Division 3-A championship.

By Emmitt's junior year, a realignment had placed Escambia High School into Division 4-A. In the first game of the season, Escambia pulled out a late win against Pensacola Woodham, the defending 4-A state champion. The Gators continued to win, going 13–1 for the year. Escambia made it to the playoffs again and this time won the state 4-A championship.

Gators head coach Dwight Thomas holds a football from the state championship game Escambia won when Emmitt was a junior.

Not only did Emmitt rush for over 100 yards in every game of the 1985 season, he went over 200 yards in seven of the games. The greatest game of his high school career came against Milton High, when he ran for 301 yards in an exciting overtime victory.

For much of Emmitt's senior season, Escambia was ranked as the Number 1 team in the entire nation. Not only that, Emmitt was regarded as the top high school player in the United States. At the end of the year, Emmitt was named the High School Player of the Year by *Parade* magazine as well as by panels of sportswriters and coaches.

The Gators were undefeated in 1986 until a late-season loss to Pensacola High. That loss kept Escambia out of the state playoffs.

Missing the playoffs was a disappointing finish for Emmitt's high school career. He finished with 106 touchdowns and averaged 7.8 yards per carry. As for his goal to run for more than 1,500 yards in a season, Emmitt had done that all four years at Escambia.

When Emmitt's high school career began, Coach Thomas had even greater expectations for him. Thomas watched Emmitt practice and told him he would gain *five miles* for the Gators. With 8,804 rushing yards in four years, Emmitt had managed the lofty goal. Only one high school player—Ken Hall of Sugar Land, Texas, in the 1950s—had ever run for more.

A portrait from Emmitt's senior year

At an awards ceremony following Emmitt's senior season, he and his parents posed for a picture.

Emmitt was also proud that he had done well in his studies. He had carried nearly a B average at Escambia and finished among the top 100 students in his class. College was definitely in Emmitt's future. Schools across the country were clamoring for him.

Emmitt thought back to his sophomore year when he had seen a teammate's recruiting letter and wished he himself would receive one. "Now I don't know what to do with all the ones I have," he said.

With his mother, Mary, by his side, Emmitt announced his intention to attend the University of Florida.

In February 1987, Coach Thomas held a lavish ceremony in the school auditorium. Nine members of the Escambia football team were signing letters of intent to play football at various colleges. The main focus was on Emmitt, who hadn't made his decision until the night before. With a large crowd looking on, Emmitt signed a letter of intent to attend the University of Florida in Gainesville.

Reflecting on Emmitt's high school career, Coach Thomas noted one quality that made the running back stand out. Emmitt was the greatest runner in the country, but he made a point of praising the offensive line that opened holes for him to run through. He also let other players know how important they were to the team.

That was the real key to Emmitt, said Coach Thomas. "He gives credit. He never takes it."

Another game, another touchdown for Emmitt, who joined
a strong University of Florida program.

Still a Gator

Emmitt was several hundred miles from home when he arrived at the University of Florida. One thing was familiar, though: the nickname of the Florida team was Gators, the same as Escambia High School's.

Emmitt wasn't at Florida only to play football. He studied hard as he worked toward a degree in therapeutic recreation. What made Emmitt different from other students, though, was his ability on the football field.

Gator coach Galen Hall wanted to bring Emmitt along slowly, allowing him time to adjust to the college game. In Florida's first game of the 1987 season, Emmitt stayed on the sideline until the fourth quarter. When he finally got in, he carried the ball five times for 16 yards. The following week, against Tulsa, Emmitt again watched the beginning of the game from the sideline. This time his chance to show what he could do came earlier—in the second quarter.

The Gators had a 3–0 lead and the ball on their 34-yard line. Quarterback Kerwin Bell handed off to Emmitt. Emmitt darted through a hole in the line and suddenly found himself in the open field. Emmitt streaked down the sideline, outrunning the one Tulsa defender who still had a shot at him. His spectacular 66-yard touchdown run sparked the Gators to an easy win over Tulsa. It also made Coach Hall rethink his strategy of bringing Emmitt along slowly.

In the Gators' third game, against Alabama, Emmitt was in the starting lineup. He put on quite a show, both for the fans at Alabama's Legion Field and a national television audience. He followed blockers when he had them and used his darting speed and elusiveness when he didn't. "You can't practice the way he runs," said Alabama coach Bill Curry. "It's a God-given talent."

By the time Emmitt sat down for the day, he had scored two touchdowns and set a school record by rushing for 224 yards. Watching Emmitt from the sidelines was Octavius Gould, a former high school All-America who had been Florida's leading rusher the year before. Gould figured he had better find another school if he hoped to get much playing time. Two days after Emmitt's big game against Alabama, Gould transferred to the University of Minnesota.

Emmitt continued to be modest about his success, and he credited the offensive line with opening big holes for him. "He compliments the people around him more than any youngster I've ever been around," said Florida offensive line coach Phil Maggio. "Those guys in front love those kinds of backs."

As a freshman, Emmitt was so effective that he earned a starting spot by the Gators' third game.

The offensive line returned the nice words after Florida's 34–3 win over Temple. Emmitt rushed for 175 yards to go over 1,000 yards in only the seventh game of the season. No other freshman in the history of major college football had reached 1,000 yards as quickly. "That was the greatest feeling I ever had as a college player—when he broke the record," said offensive lineman David Williams. "It was so great to be a part of it all. I felt like I was the one who was running the ball."

Emmitt finished the regular season with 1,341 yards rushing. He had another 128 against UCLA in the Aloha Bowl. He was named Freshman of the Year by United Press International and *The Sporting News* and finished ninth in the voting for the Heisman Trophy, which is given to the best player in college football. Herschel Walker of Georgia was the only other freshman ever to crack the top 10 in the Heisman balloting.

"We expected he was going to be good, but we never expected those kinds of numbers that fast," said Coach Hall. "He was just very confident. He believed in himself."

Emmitt and the Gators got off to a great start in 1988. In the fourth game of the season, against Mississippi State, Emmitt broke a pair of tackles on a 12-yard touchdown run. Then, in the second quarter, he injured his calf and appeared to be done for the day.

He returned to the game in the third quarter, though. Florida had a 10–0 lead but was pinned deep in its own territory. Emmitt moved the Gators out of there. He took a handoff, slashed through the line, broke away from a defender, and sprinted down the left sideline for a 96-yard touchdown, the longest in the school's history.

The following week, Emmitt ran for 132 yards against Louisiana State to go over 2,000 yards for his college career. Counting the bowl game against UCLA, it was the eighth-straight game in which Emmitt had rushed for at least 100 yards.

It looked like he would extend that streak in the Gators' next game, against Memphis State. But after racking up 89 yards, he had to leave the game in the third quarter with a sprained knee. The injury was serious enough to keep Emmitt from playing in the next two games.

The injury cost Emmitt a chance at winning the Heisman Trophy as a sophomore. It also hurt the Gators. Florida had won its first five games and was ranked nationally. After the injury to Emmitt, the Gators lost five of their last six regular-season games.

They still received an invitation to a bowl game, despite their mediocre record. In the All-American Bowl against Illinois, Emmitt rushed for 159 yards. He had two touchdowns, including one on a 55-yard run, and was named the game's Most Valuable Player.

Although Emmitt battled leg and knee injuries during his sophomore season, he still managed to gain more than 100 yards in seven games.

The 14–10 victory was a bright finish to an otherwise disappointing season. Emmitt looked forward to his junior year. If he could stay healthy and play every game, he knew he'd have a real chance at the Heisman Trophy. The Gators would also have a chance to be among the nation's top teams.

The Gators had a new offensive coordinator, Whitey Jordan, in 1989. Jordan had coached NFL superstar Eric Dickerson at Southern Methodist University. "Eric was faster, bigger," said Jordan, when asked to compare the two running backs, "but Emmitt has more moves. He knows how to make people miss, so nobody gets a solid lick on him."

Florida lost its opening game but won the next six. In the midst of this winning streak, though, came turmoil that would tarnish the season. The day after the Gators beat Louisiana State for their fourth win, Coach Galen Hall abruptly resigned. There were charges that Hall had given money to a player and some assistant coaches, which was against National Collegiate Athletic Association (NCAA) rules.

Even with the distraction of changing coaches, Emmitt had a big game against Vanderbilt the following Saturday. He rushed for 202 yards, giving him more than 3,000 for his college career. Florida won the game, 34–11, and was ranked Number 25 in the country.

Then came more trouble. Quarterbacks Kyle Morris and Shane Matthews were suspended for the rest of the season because they had placed bets on college football games early in the year.

The Gators kept plugging away, despite all the problems. With the team's top two quarterbacks gone, Florida would have to rely even more on Emmitt and the running game. Emmitt didn't let the Gators down. In the next game, against New Mexico, Emmitt ran for 316 yards and scored three touchdowns. One of the scores came on a 72-yard run that broke the school career record for rushing yards and touchdowns. Both records had been held by Neal Anderson, who became an outstanding running back for the

Chicago Bears. After the game, Anderson called Emmitt to congratulate him.

The game against New Mexico was the high point of the season for Florida. The Gators lost three of the last four regular-season games, then were trounced by Washington in the Freedom Bowl.

Emmitt had produced terrific numbers his junior year. He led the Southeastern Conference (SEC) with 1,599 yards rushing on 284 carries—a 5.6 average. In addition to being voted the SEC Player of the Year, he was named All-America at running back. Despite the great statistics, he finished only seventh in the balloting for the Heisman Trophy. The controversy surrounding the Florida football team had taken its toll on everyone, including Emmitt. Even though Emmitt was never accused of breaking rules, many sports experts thought the team's troubles hurt him in the Heisman voting.

The fallout wasn't over either. The NCAA was about to place the Florida football team on probation because of the rules violations. That would mean no bowl game and no appearances on national television for the Gators during Emmitt's senior season.

At least Emmitt had other options. For the first time, underclassmen (juniors and younger) would be eligible for the NFL draft. In early 1990, Emmitt announced he was going to skip his senior season and enter the NFL.

After three seasons, Emmitt left the University of Florida with 58 school records.

In only three years on the Gators team, Emmitt had set 58 Florida single-game, single-season, or career records. Undoubtedly, he would have set even more records had he played his fourth season. Emmitt's parents weren't as concerned about him setting more records as they were about him leaving school before graduating. Emmitt promised Mary and Emmitt II that he would get his degree before marrying or buying a house.

For the time being, though, he was going to be a pro football player.

Dallas coaches knew Emmitt's ability to run the ball and find the end zone could help turn the Cowboys around.

Super Seasons

Several professional scouts and coaches thought Emmitt wasn't big enough or fast enough to play in the NFL. Dallas coach Jimmy Johnson knew how good Emmitt was. Johnson had coached at the University of Miami, and the Hurricanes were among college teams recruiting Emmitt out of high school.

Johnson hoped this time he'd be able to get Emmitt. "There were all these people saying 'He's too slow' or 'He's too small.' All I know is that every time I saw a film of him, he was running 50, 60, 70, 80 yards for a touchdown," said Johnson. "That looked pretty good to me."

Dallas had the 21st pick in the 1990 NFL draft. The Cowboys' staff hoped teams would shy away from Emmitt so he'd still be available for them. Midway through the first round of the draft, Emmitt still had not been picked. Coach Johnson decided not to wait any longer. He traded with the Pittsburgh Steelers, who had the 17th selection, then used that pick to draft Emmitt.

Dallas owner Jerry Jones was jubilant about landing Emmitt so late in the round. He told reporters the Cowboys had rated Emmitt as the fourth-best player available. Later, he wished he hadn't said that. When the time came to discuss a contract, Emmitt and his agent requested to be paid like the fourth-best player Jones had said he was. Jones wanted to pay closer to what the 16th and 18th picks were getting.

The two sides also disagreed on how long the contract should run. Emmitt was confident he'd quickly become valuable to the team. He wanted a contract for only three years, so he would then be free to ask for an even better contract. The Cowboys wanted Emmitt locked up for five years.

Emmitt wasn't going to accept a contract he didn't like and was even willing to sit out a year of football. During his holdout, he returned to Gainesville and registered for classes at the University of Florida. He probably wouldn't be allowed to continue playing college football, but he could at least work toward his degree.

Emmitt finally got the three-year contract he wanted from Dallas. He missed all of training camp, though, and reported to the Cowboys only a few days before the season opener. He barely played in the first two games. He quickly learned the Dallas offense, however, and began to get more opportunities.

In only his fifth NFL game, he had 23 carries for 121 yards against the Tampa Bay Buccaneers. In the ensuing games, though, he didn't get nearly as many chances to carry the ball.

Meanwhile, the Cowboys struggled and had only 3 wins after 10 games. Emmitt felt the problem was that he wasn't getting enough chances to run the ball and pick up the rushing yards the offense needed. He talked to the team's backfield coach and then made an even bolder move. He spoke on a radio sports show and said he should get the ball more.

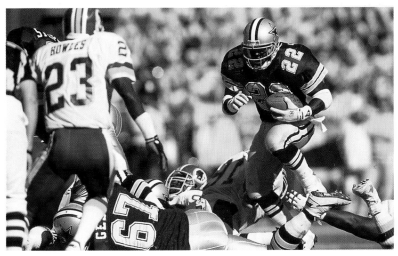

Emmitt wasn't afraid to take responsibility as a rookie. He urged the Cowboys' coaching staff to put more emphasis on the running game.

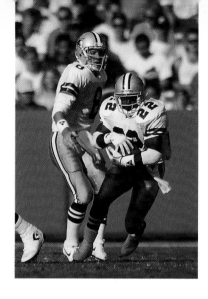

Emmitt takes the handoff from quarterback Troy Aikman during Emmitt's rookie year. Both players proved vital to Dallas's success.

The move worked. The Dallas coaching staff decided to give him the chance to either prove himself or fail. It was the type of challenge that always brought out the best in Emmitt. He had at least 20 carries in each of the next four Cowboys' games and rushed for over 100 yards in two of them. Dallas won all four of those games. Emmitt had shown how big his role was in the team's success.

The Cowboys finished the season at 7–9. Their record wasn't good enough for a playoff spot, but it was a big improvement over the 1–15 record of the previous season.

In 1991 Johnson was ready to let Emmitt lead the running game. He carried the ball 365 times, more than any other player in the league. He also led the NFL with 1,563 yards, the first Cowboy ever to be the league's top rusher. Not only did he gain a lot of yards, Emmitt was such a threat as a runner that he opened up the Dallas passing game. Quarterback Troy Aikman and wide receiver Michael Irvin became one of the top passing combinations in the game, and they gave Emmitt a lot of the credit for their success.

Emmitt earned a starting spot in the NFL Pro Bowl, the league's all-star game, for his outstanding season. More importantly, the Cowboys improved their record to 11–5 and made the playoffs for the first time since 1985. They beat the Chicago Bears in the first round of the playoffs before losing to the Detroit Lions.

The Cowboys were encouraged by their improvement—so encouraged that they set their sights even higher. Their goal for the 1992 season would be the world championship.

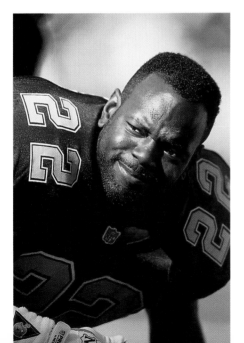

At the start of the 1992 season, Emmitt's future was looking great, and the Cowboys were aiming for the top.

Dallas opened its 1992 season against the defending Super Bowl winners, the Washington Redskins. Emmitt had a big first game, running for 140 yards as the Cowboys won easily. As the season progressed, the league's top defenses couldn't contain Emmitt. He rushed for 167 yards against the Philadelphia Eagles. The last time anyone ran for more than 100 yards against the Eagles was in 1989.

Although he was having a great season, Emmitt trailed Barry Foster of the Pittsburgh Steelers for the NFL rushing lead going into the final week of games. With 131 yards in his last game of the regular season, Emmitt shot past Foster to win another rushing title.

Emmitt was even more excited about leading the league for the second straight year than he had been the first time. "This title was a lot sweeter than last season because it proves last season wasn't a fluke," he said. The 1,713 yards he gained in 1992 set a Dallas record, breaking the mark held by Tony Dorsett.

Emmitt stayed hot through the playoffs. He had 114 yards in a win over the Philadelphia Eagles and matched that number as the Cowboys beat San Francisco in the NFC title game. Dallas's next opponent would be the Buffalo Bills—in the Super Bowl.

A number of Cowboys had big games as Dallas easily beat the Bills, 52–17. Quarterback Troy Aikman was the game's Most Valuable Player, but Emmitt did well too. He ran for over 100 yards and one touchdown.

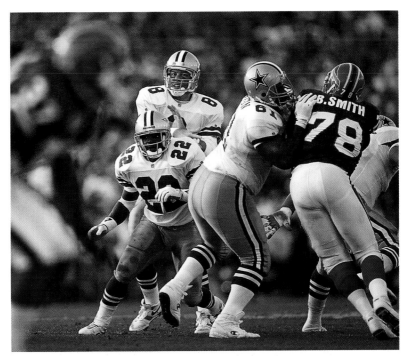

With Troy in the pocket, Emmitt gets ready to block any defender who rushes the quarterback.

In a span of just three years, Dallas had gone from being the league's doormat to the best team in football. Now other teams would be gunning for the Cowboys. They'd have to work hard to stay the best, and Emmitt knew it.

"When you've reached the top," he said, "you either stay there or you go down."

That would be true for both Emmitt and the Dallas Cowboys.

Without a contract for the 1993–1994 season, Emmitt was prepared to walk away from the game for a year.

Taking Care of Business

Emmitt's contract with the Cowboys expired after the 1992 season, and he wouldn't accept the new one the Cowboys offered. Emmitt had become one of the top running backs in football, and he expected to be paid more.

Owner Jerry Jones hoped to sign Emmitt for less money than his star running back wanted, but Emmitt wouldn't give in. He refused to attend training camp without a contract, and his holdout extended into the season.

Jones openly questioned whether the Cowboys really needed Emmitt, and he quickly found out that they did. Without Emmitt, Dallas lost its first two games. The second loss was against Buffalo, the team the Cowboys had beaten so badly in the Super Bowl eight months before. In the game, Derrick Lassic, Emmitt's backup at running back, fumbled twice. The poor game was enough to convince Jones he needed to give in and offer Emmitt more money.

The fact that Emmitt was tough at contract time was not surprising. He approaches the business of football as intensely as he plays the game.

During his holdout, Emmitt passed much of the time in Pensacola, working at his sports memorabilia store. Early in his career, Emmitt had set up his own company—Emmitt Inc.—for various business dealings. One part of Emmitt Inc. is the Pensacola store, called 1st and 10. It's a family operation, managed by Emmitt's parents and his older sister, Marsha.

Mary Smith, Emmitt's mother, helps run 1st and 10.

After signing autographs in exchange for food, clothing, and toys, Emmitt delivers the goods to people living in an impoverished area of Dallas.

By this time, Emmitt had increased his role in community affairs. He started the Emmitt Smith Charity Golf Tournament in his hometown to raise money for organizations in the Pensacola area. The Emmitt Smith Foundation extends his efforts in charity work. Emmitt also spends time with teens and is active in antidrug campaigns.

"I'm more proud of that than anything else he's done," Emmitt II said of his son's community work.

After winning his contract battle, Emmitt joined the Cowboys for the third game of the 1993 season. His teammates were thrilled to see him again. Nate Newton said having Emmitt back in the lineup was "just like the good old days. When Emmitt runs and he hits the line, you feel something powerful crunching up in there. When he did it for the first time, I said to him, 'Welcome back, baby!'"

Emmitt needed a few games to regain his form. When he hit his stride, opposing teams were in trouble. On a frigid Halloween Night in Philadelphia, he set a club single-game record by rushing for 237 yards.

Emmitt carries the ball in his first game back during the 1993 season.

Emmitt finished the regular season with his great performance at Giants Stadium—the game in which he separated his shoulder. The shoulder injury continued to bother him in the postseason. Even though Emmitt was playing injured, the Cowboys beat Green Bay and San Francisco to return to the Super Bowl for the second year in a row. Emmitt was ready for a big game.

The Cowboys played Buffalo again, and this time the Bills did better. They shut down the Dallas offense and held a 13–6 lead at halftime. Offensive coordinator Norv Turner felt Emmitt would be the key to the team's success in the second half. "Just get him the ball," Turner said.

Before Emmitt could do anything, though, the Dallas defense came through with a big play. Leon Lett forced a fumble, and safety James Washington returned it for a touchdown to tie the game. The Cowboy defense then stopped Buffalo on its next possession, forcing the Bills to punt.

With the offense finally on the field, Dallas was ready to put Norv Turner's strategy into play. Emmitt would run the ball until the Bills showed they could stop him. Starting from their own 36-yard line, the Cowboys gave Emmitt the ball on the next six plays. He covered 46 yards, advancing Dallas to the Buffalo 18. After a 3-yard screen pass to Daryl "Moose" Johnston, the call went to Emmitt again.

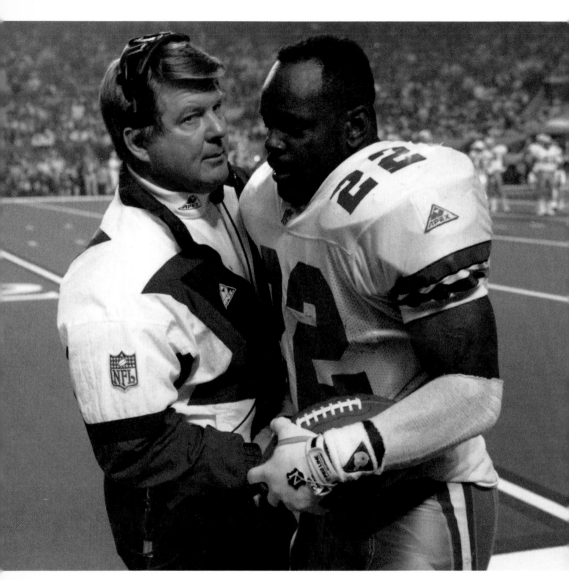

After scoring in the third quarter of Super Bowl XXVIII, Emmitt
gets a hug on the sideline from coach Jimmy Johnson.

This time he powered through the right side for a 15-yard touchdown run. The Cowboys led, 20–13.

The Cowboys clung to their one-touchdown lead into the fourth quarter. They centered another drive around Emmitt and got within a yard of the goal line. At fourth down with a yard to go, the coaches had to make a decision. Coach Jimmy Johnson had so much confidence in Emmitt that he passed up an easy field goal and went for the bigger score. His risk paid off. The Bills still couldn't stop Emmitt, who ran for his second touchdown and put the Cowboys ahead by 14 points.

Dallas cruised the rest of the way and won its second-straight Super Bowl. Emmitt finished with 132 yards rushing. It was the 100th game of his football career in which he rushed for at least 100 yards. For his performance, he was named the Most Valuable Player of the Super Bowl.

Injuries again hampered Emmitt during the 1994 season.

Back in the Saddle

After the season, Emmitt had surgery to repair his shoulder. In 1994 he had problems with another part of his body. Injured hamstrings—the group of muscles at the backside of the upper leg—kept him out of one game and part of four more during the regular season. Then, in the team's first playoff game, he injured the hamstring muscles again. The Cowboys still won, but Emmitt wasn't at full strength in the NFC Championship Game. With Emmitt hurting, the Cowboys lost to the San Francisco 49ers.

The injuries ended two strings: Emmitt's streak of three-consecutive rushing titles and the Cowboys' run of two-straight Super Bowl championships. Head coach Barry Switzer, who had replaced Jimmy Johnson following the 1993 season, was determined to make Dallas the world champion again in 1995. Emmitt and the rest of the Cowboys were just as determined.

The first time Emmitt touched the ball in the 1995 season opener against the New York Giants, he ran 60 yards for a touchdown. He was just warming up. Emmitt finished the game with four touchdowns as Dallas won, 35–0.

He continued on his touchdown roll through the following months. In the next-to-last game of the season, Emmitt scored his 24th touchdown, tying the NFL single-season record. Dallas's final game of the year was at Arizona. The Cowboys had a comfortable lead in the fourth quarter, but Emmitt hadn't scored.

Emmitt squeezes through a hole in the first game of the 1995 season.

Emmitt's teammates congratulate him for setting a new NFL record for most touchdowns in a season.

His teammates weren't ready to let up yet. With less than six minutes left in the game, Emmitt finally carried the ball into the end zone for his record-breaking touchdown.

Dallas finished with a 12–4 won-lost record, the best in the NFC. Emmitt rushed for 1,773 yards. For the fourth time in five seasons, he was the NFL's top rusher.

Emmitt and the Cowboys were almost back to where they wanted to be. They easily defeated Philadelphia in a divisional playoff game but had trouble with Green Bay for the conference championship.

The game was tied in the second quarter, and the Cowboys had the ball on their own 1-yard line. Emmitt quickly got them out of the hole with a 25-yard run. He carried the ball five more times, finally scoring a touchdown to put Dallas ahead at halftime.

By the fourth quarter, though, the Packers had a 27–24 lead. Emmitt changed that with another touchdown run. He also scored a third touchdown to put the game out of reach.

The Cowboys were back in the Super Bowl. They faced the Pittsburgh Steelers, who did a good job of bottling up the Cowboy offense. But the Dallas defense came up with some big plays, including two interceptions by cornerback Larry Brown. Emmitt scored a touchdown on both Cowboy drives following the interceptions, and Dallas won the game, 27–17.

The Cowboys were back on top. But, as always, they want more.

As Emmitt becomes more and more successful on the field, people continue to want more from him. He is enormously popular, so many companies pay Emmitt to be in their advertisements. Coca-Cola, Reebok, and Starter are among the companies that use Emmitt to endorse their products.

Despite all his success, Emmitt remains firmly grounded in the values his parents taught him. "I credit his upbringing for the way he conducts himself," said an assistant coach with the Cowboys. "He has been brought up to be a winner all his life and to care. When he talks about feelings for others, he means it."

The Cowboys were back on top, beating Pittsburgh in Super Bowl XXX.

Mary Smith spruces up Emmitt's cap on graduation day.

Emmitt agrees and adds, "There is nothing that I am today that I would be without my family."

After winning three Super Bowls and making more than enough money to secure his future, Emmitt kept the promise he made to his parents. He had taken enough college classes and earned his bachelor's degree in May 1996 from the University of Florida.

In football, Emmitt progresses toward another goal: surpassing Walter Payton's career rushing record of 16,726 yards. Breaking that, says Emmitt, "would set me apart from everybody else.

"I'm chasing after legends," he adds, "after Walter Payton and Tony Dorsett and Jim Brown and Eric Dickerson, after guys who made history. When my career's over, I want to have the new kids say, 'Boy, we have to chase a legend to be the best.'

"And they'll mean Emmitt Smith."

EMMITT SMITH'S
FOOTBALL STATISTICS

University of Florida Gators

Year	Games	Rushes	Rushing Yards	Rushing Touchdowns	Passes Caught	Receiving Yards	Receiving Touchdowns
1987	11	229	1,341	13	25	184	0
1988	9	187	988	9	10	72	0
1989	11	284	1,599	14	21	207	1
Totals	31	700	3,928	36	56	463	1

College Highlights:

Freshman of the Year, 1987.
All-American Bowl Most Valuable Player, 1988.
Southeastern Conference (SEC) rushing leader, 1989.
SEC Player of the Year, 1989.
All-SEC, 1987, 1988, 1989.
All-America, 1987, 1988, 1989.
First team All-America, 1989.

Dallas Cowboys—Regular Season

Year	Games	Rushes	Rushing Yards	Rushing Touchdowns	Passes Caught	Receiving Yards	Receiving Touchdowns
1990	16	241	937	11	24	228	0
1991	16	365	1,563	12	49	258	1
1992	16	373	1,713	18	59	335	1
1993	14	283	1,486	9	57	414	1
1994	15	368	1,484	21	50	341	1
1995	16	377	1,773	25	62	375	0
Totals	93	2,007	8,956	96	301	1,951	4

Career Highlights:

NFL Most Valuable Player, 1993.
Offensive Rookie of the Year, 1990.
Super Bowl Most Valuable Player, 1993 season.
NFL rushing leader, 1991, 1992, 1993, 1995.
Named to play in Pro Bowl, 1990, 1991, 1992, 1993, 1994, 1995.
NFL record for touchdowns in a season, 25 in 1995.
All-NFL, 1992, 1993, 1994, 1995.

ACKNOWLEDGMENTS

Photographs are reproduced by permission of: Mike Powell/Allsport, p. 1; Doug Pensinger/Allsport, pp. 2–3, 41; REUTERS/Ray Stubblebine/Archive Photos, pp. 6, 10; SportsChrome East/West/Robert Tringali Jr., pp. 9, 42, 45; Gary McCracken, pp. 14, 22, 24, 26, 48; Pensacola News Journal, pp. 19; Pensacola News Journal/Dale Bass, p. 20; Dwight Thomas, p. 25; Allen Dean Steele/Allsport, pp. 28, 34, 37; SportsChrome East/West/David L. Johnson, p. 31; Jonathan Daniel/Allsport, p. 38; Otto Greule/Allsport, p. 43; Sue Allen Camp/Allsport, p. 46; Tim Sharp, p. 49; Tim Defrisco/Allsport, p. 50; Reuters/Bettman, p. 52; Al Bello/Allsport, p. 54; Sports-Chrome East/West/Rich Kane, p. 56; Jamie Squire/Allsport, p. 57; SportsChrome East/West, p. 59; University of Florida, Sports Information Dept., p. 60; and Stephen Dunn/Allsport, p. 63.

Front cover photograph reproduced by permission of Mike Powell/Allsport. Back cover photograph reproduced by permission of SportsChrome East/West/Vincent Manniello.

Index